TOXIC PARENTING

Dear friends and fans,

I just wanted to take a moment to express my heartfelt gratitude for all the love and support you've shown me over the years. Your unwavering support has been a source of inspiration and motivation for me, and I feel incredibly blessed to have you in my life.

I know that I wouldn't be where I am today without your encouragement and kindness, and I am truly grateful for everything you've done for me. Thank you for being there for me through thick and thin, and for believing in me even when I didn't believe in myself.

I hope that I can continue to inspire and entertain you in the years to come, and that we can share many more happy memories together. Thank you again for your support, and know that I am always here for you, too.

With love and appreciation,

HANIA MUJAHID

*Message for you if you are passing through **TOXIC PARENTING**:*

My dear friend,

I want you to know that I am here for you, no matter what. I know that things may seem tough right now, but please know that you are not alone. I care about you deeply, and I am here to support you in any way that I can.

Remember that it's okay to feel overwhelmed, and that it's okay to ask for help. You are strong and capable, but you don't have to go through this alone. I am here to listen, to comfort, and to help you find your way through the darkness.

Please don't give up hope, even when things seem impossible. There is always a light at the end of the tunnel, and I believe that you will emerge from this stronger and more resilient than ever before.

I love you, and I am here for you, always.

With all my heart,

    HANIA MUJAHID

"Toxic parenting is like a heavy rain that falls on a young sapling. The tree may bend and sway, but it will never break. And when the storm passes, the tree will grow stronger, its roots deep and resilient, reaching for the sun."

LIFE CHAPTER

Zohi! A 13-year-old girl. Having no friends just living her life.

 "does she feel bad for herself"? I don't know about her but I feel bad for her.

Zohi was attending a maths lecture. it was raining outside. she was looking out of the window. she was thinking about something and she was lost in that thought.

Teacher: Be attentive! I will not repeat my words. you have to understand the lecture so it will not be a problem for you later.

She start paying attention in class and she was understanding everything that the teacher was saying. Maths lecture ended ***bell rang**.* Everyone was in a rush because it was off time but she was so quiet and doing her work slowly because there was nothing special at the home. she was not excited about anything because she knows what would happen when she will reach home. She packed her bag and walk towards home. She reached home

She saw her parents were fighting. she ignored them and went straight into her room. After some minutes her parents stop fighting and her mother called her to join them for food.

She comes to the table and her mother handover food to her. Her mother cooked brinjal which she use to hate the most but her mother didn't know about that because she never paid attention to her. Without saying a word she just ate her food and went into her room to do her homework. she was all depressed because she really don't have any kind of friends. She just laid down on her bed and started using her phone but later she get annoyed of her phone. she put the phone aside and start doing her homework after finishing her homework. she event out of her room. She saw her mother was watching a drama on the TV. she asked her mother let's talk about something. pay attention to me.

Her mother: You can go out. We will talk about something later. I am not free right now.

NEXT DAY:
She was coming back from her school. She saw her father fighting with someone on the road. she ran towards him and try to stop them but her father pushed her away. She got injured but her father didn't notice that she stood up and walk towards her house. on the way, she met a stranger who was sitting under the street light. she sat beside her. That stranger looked towards her and ignored her.

Zohi: Hello my name is Zohi! I'm coming back from my school.

Stranger: hello my name is Lisa.

Zohi: I was going back to my house but I don't want to go back because I know what is going to happen. it makes me so depressed. I don't want to go back to that house. I just want to leave that house and go far away from them.

Lisa was looking at her curiously.

Lisa: why are you telling me this I didn't ask you about anything. you just came and sat here.

Zohi: I was just so depressed. I want to say something. I wanted to talk to someone. I just met you. you're nothing special.

She picks her bag and walk home. She was finding her keys suddenly her mother open the door and pick up her bag and put it aside and welcome her. she was surprised at what is happening because her mother never treated her like that before she was curious so that's why she asked her mother *" why are you doing this"?* her mother replied *"I and your father are getting a divorce and you have to choose with whom you want to live"*

She was shocked and ask when it happened. Her mother said ***it is just none of your business. you just have to reply to whom you will choose?*** she was stunned for the moment. She doesn't know whom she should choose because both of them never treated her well. She was stunned and went into her room and set on the bed and thinking about it. Suddenly a bell rang and her father came. He was apologizing for something but she didn't understand what is happening. she came out of the Room. Her father ask her the same question ***"whom you will choose"*** she said ***I will choose mother.*** What happened today melts her heart she remember how her father pushed her and didn't care about her and just remember how her mother welcome her.

Her father disappointed slap on her face and left the house. Her mother hugged her and said ***it is okay just forget about it*** then she went into her room and thought about her decision.

The next morning when she woke up there was a man inside their house she ask her mother **"who is he"** her mother replied **he is my lawyer and I hired him for your custody and to proceed with my divorce case**.

She quietly left the house and she saw her father wandering with a lady.

, **"I think my decision is correct"**.
said zohi

Her mother got her custody after time passed She start to realize that she had made the wrong decision because her mother starts scolding her over the little things and started ignoring her again. she was just learning from her mother how to be irresponsible and she start hating her father and mother both and decided to choose her path. Next morning when her Mother   went to wake up her but she notices that she was not there and even her belongings were not there.

On the other side, we saw that she was bordering a train and moving out of the station. she settled there she bought a new house there. She does Part time Jobs and she had a hobby of paintings

after 5 years

suddenly the bell rang
door opened
her mother was shocked and sad Zohi *what are you doing*? *why you left me 5 years ago.?*

Zohi: I am just here to look over you. I was just worried about you and father. I have many things to tell you. Even if you never care about me but still I miss you. I have something to tell you that I have been doing a job and I have saved a lot of money. and I am going out of the country and I'll forget everything that happened in my past. So before going I want to meet you and dad.

She called her father and ask him to join the dinner and told him everything. Her father came with his wife but zohi said that she only want you to come I don't want your wife to come in. They were sitting at

the dining table eating food quietly and took her bag and take out some money and said *this is some money I want to give you before I leave as a gift*. Her parents took the money. They both at the same time asked *how much money do you have.* She replied I *have 6 billion in my bank account I start my business painting and I won the lottery that's why I have this much money...*

They both look shocked...

Her mother stand up and went to the kitchen. She bring her a glass of juice and there was something strange. she drink the juice and she was feeling anxious suddenly she felt like she was dying.

 !! she died!!

Her mother: that's all is. We will use that whole money

laughing

They both handshake...

Zohi opened her eye... They were in shock... She pretended to be dead because she saw her mother putting poison in the Juice...

when I choose my father I feel bad for you mother but when I choose you mother I feel bad for father. so I decided to love both of you equally that was hard for me to choose one of you but you both never love me. you both are involved in the conspiracy. I didn't drink that because I saw you put poison in that. She said

Crying Hard...

She felt Distortion in her breathing and she was losing all her power. she fell because the food she ate was poisoned.. when her mother went to bring the juice her father put the poison in the food...

She died!!!

THANKS

 I want to take a moment to thank you for reading my book, even though it had a sad ending. I know that it can be difficult to read stories that touch on sensitive or emotional topics, and I am grateful for your willingness to engage with the material.

As an author, I believe that it is important to tell stories that reflect the complexity of the human experience, even when that experience is painful or difficult to confront. And while I am sorry that my book may have left you feeling sad or overwhelmed, I hope that it has also helped you to see the beauty and resilience that can emerge from even the darkest of moments.

Thank you again for taking the time to read my book. Your support means everything to me, and I am deeply grateful for your kindness and generosity.

With warmest regards,

HANIA MUJAHID

SOCIAL MEDIA

INSTAGRAM : arcane_rosie

YOU TUBE :Aracne_rosie

TIK TOK : arcane_rosie

MEDIUM : Arcane Rosie

INKITT : ArcaneRosie

WEB NOVEL : ArcaneRosie

MY INTRODUCTION:

HANIA MUJAHID, A TEENAGER WHO LOVES TO READ AND WRITES . I ALWAYS WANTED TO ME A WRITER AND I THINK ITS MY TIME. MY INSPIRATION! TBH I LEARNED HOW TO FULFILL YOUR DREAM FROM KOREAN DREAMS. AS THEY WORK HARD TO ARCHEIVE THEIR GOAL INSPIRE ME. I GOT MOTIVATED AND NOW I AM ON THIS PLATEFORM. <3

MY UPCOMING STORY

I NEED YOU TO LOVE ME LITTLE LOUDER TODAY

GENRE OF MY UPCOMING STOR:

- ❖ *THRILLER*
- ❖ *ROMANCE*
- ❖ *MYSTERY*

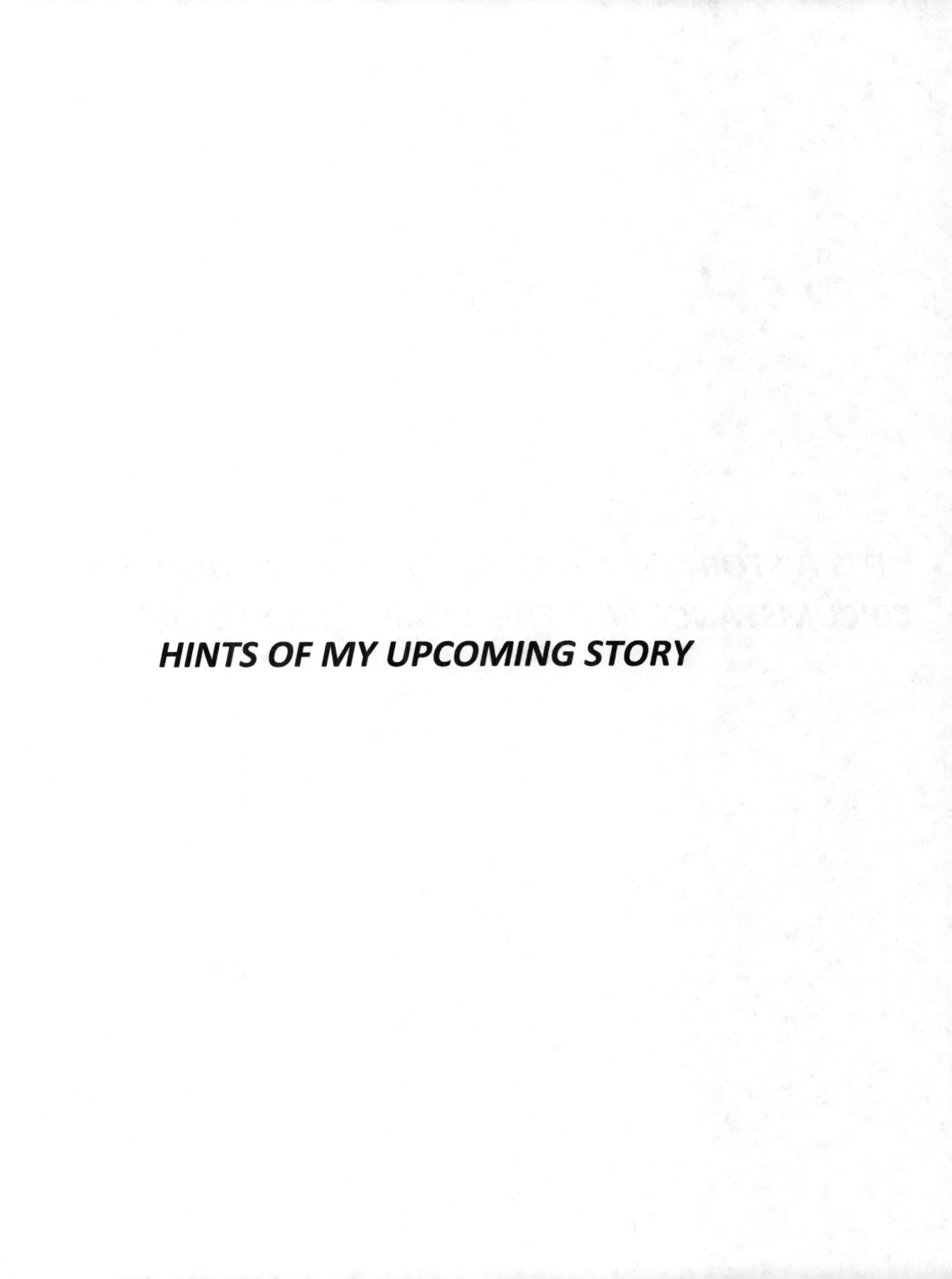
HINTS OF MY UPCOMING STORY

IT'S A STORY OF A GIRL AND BOY AND THEIR LIFE CIRCUMSTANCE AND THEIR HAPPY OR SAD LIFE.

ALWAYS BE HAPPY

9 798853 659629